DK eyewonder

Volcanoes

LONDON, NEW YORK, MUNICH,
MELBOURNE, and DELHI

Written and edited by Lisa Magloff
Designed by Laura Roberts
Publishing manager Susan Leonard
Managing art editor Clare Shedden
US editor Margaret Parrish
Picture researcher Sarah Pownall
Production Shivani Pandey
DTP designer Almudena Díaz
Consultant Chris Pellant

REVISED EDITION
DK UK
Senior editor Caroline Stamps
Senior art editor Rachael Grady
Jacket design Natasha Rees
Producer (print production) Rita Sinha
Producers (pre-production)
Francesca Wardell, Rachel Ng
Publisher Andrew Macintyre

DK INDIA
Senior editor Priyanka Nath
Senior art editor Rajnish Kashyap
Assistant editor Deeksha Saikia
Assistant art editor Dhirendra Singh
Managing editor Alka Thakur Hazarika
Managing art editor Romi Chakraborty
DTP designer Anita Yadav
Picture researcher Sumedha Chopra

First American Edition, 2003
This American Edition, 2013
Published in the United States by
DK Publishing
375 Hudson Street
New York, New York 10014
13 14 15 16 17 10 9 8 7 6 5 4 3 2 1
001—192751—05/2013

A catalog record for this book is available
from the Library of Congress.
ISBN 978-1-4654-0909-6
DK books are available at special discounts when
purchased in bulk for sales promotions, premiums, fund-
raising, or educational use. For details, contact: DK
Publishing Special Markets, 375 Hudson Street, New York,
New York 10014 or SpecialSales@dk.com.

Color reproduction by Scanhouse, Malaysia
Printed and bound in China by Hung Hing.

Discover more at
www.dk.com

Contents

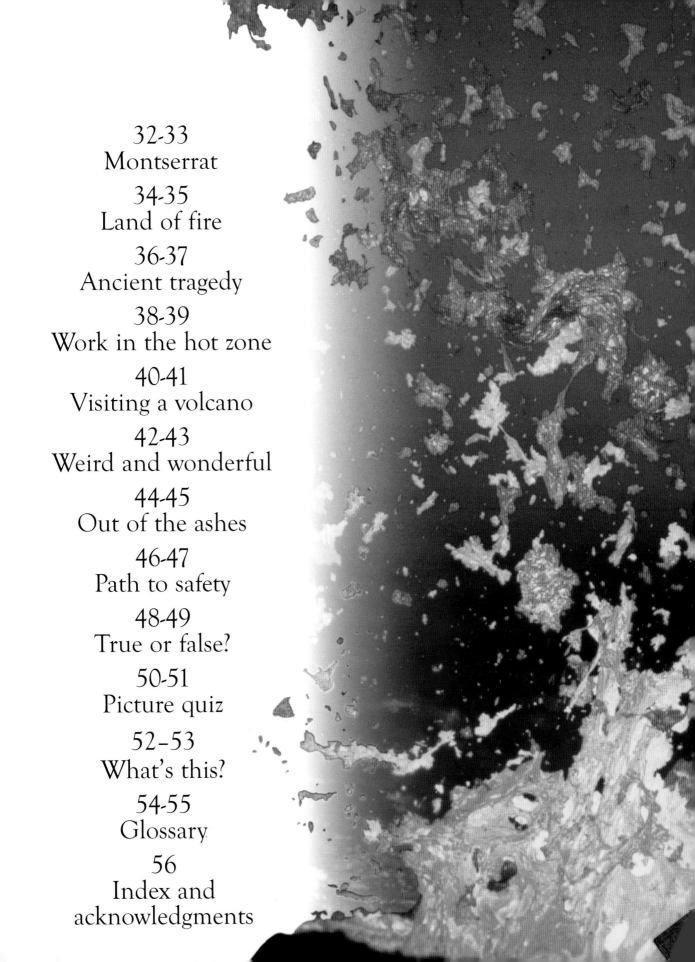

Spitting fire

Deep under the Earth, rocks melt into a thick liquid called magma. When the pressure in the Earth's crust builds up, the magma explodes in a volcanic eruption.

As it rises, the magma breaks up rocks near the surface, which can cause earthquakes.

Heat and fire
The red-hot molten rock that explodes out of a volcano is beautiful but deadly. It is so hot that it can melt steel.

Earth's crust
The Earth's crust is made of...
Loose rocks and dirt.

Sedimentary rocks made from bits of rock stuck together.

Igneous rocks made from magma that has cooled.

Metamorphic rocks made from squashed rocks.

Once it has risen to the surface, magma is called lava.

Ready to blow

The force of an exploding volcano can throw lava more than 2,000 ft (610 m) into the air. Lava, gas, and huge chunks of rock are all ejected from the volcano.

Lower mantle

Outer core

Inner core

The Earth's crust is a layer of rock between 3½ and 42 miles (5.6 and 68 km) thick.

The layer of moving rock below the crust is the mantle.

Peeling away the layers

The Earth is made up of many layers, just like an onion. Instead of onion skin, the Earth's layers are made of rock and metals.

Deep in the Earth

Below the mantle is the outer core. This layer is made up of iron and nickel that has melted. Below this is the inner core, where temperatures reach 8,130°F (500°C).

Jigsaw Earth

The Earth's crust is broken into pieces called plates, which are always moving. Sometimes we can feel the movement in an earthquake. Many volcanoes occur in places where plates bump together or pull apart.

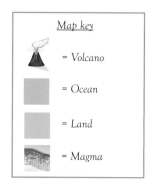
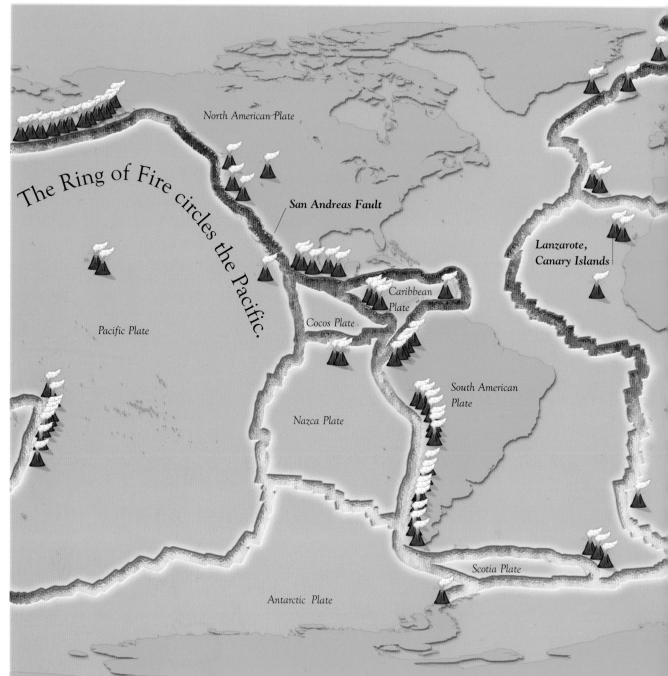

North American Plate

The Ring of Fire circles the Pacific.

San Andreas Fault

Lanzarote, Canary Islands

Pacific Plate

Caribbean Plate

Cocos Plate

South American Plate

Nazca Plate

Scotia Plate

Antarctic Plate

Visible fault

The San Andreas Fault in California is a place where two plates slide against each other. The plates move about ½ in (1 cm) a year.

All in a row

On Lanzarote, Canary Islands, magma bubbles up in places where plates break apart. These weak spots are called fissures.

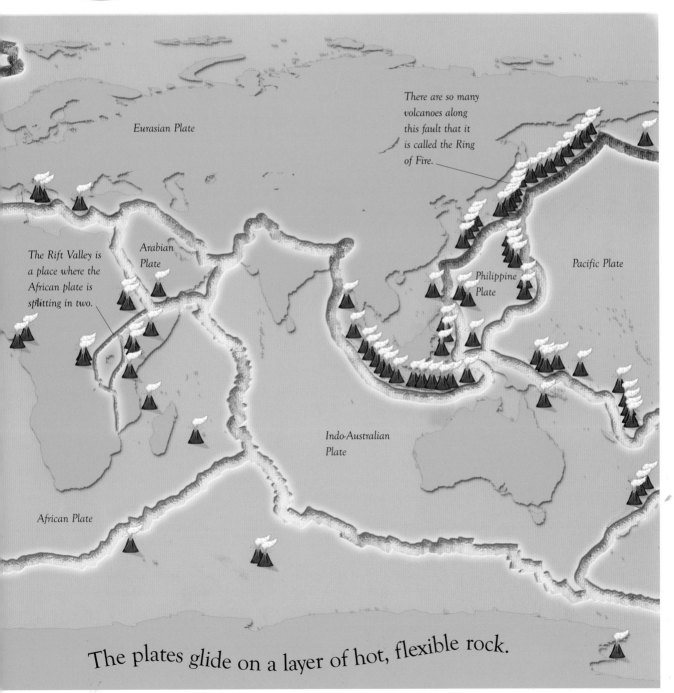

Eurasian Plate

There are so many volcanoes along this fault that it is called the Ring of Fire.

The Rift Valley is a place where the African plate is splitting in two.

Arabian Plate

Pacific Plate

Philippine Plate

Indo-Australian Plate

African Plate

The plates glide on a layer of hot, flexible rock.

Hot spots

In some places, the Earth's crust is thin enough for a column of hot magma to burn a hole and create a volcano. These places are called hot spots.

Hot water spot

Yellowstone Park in Wyoming is located over a hot spot. Two million years ago a volcano erupted here. Today, underground heat fuels the park's 10,000 geysers.

Lava erupts from Piton de la Fournaise in many places at the same time.

Island of fire

Réunion Island, in the Indian Ocean, contains one of the world's most active volcanoes—Piton de la Fournaise. Réunion Island formed over a hot spot about 5 million years ago.

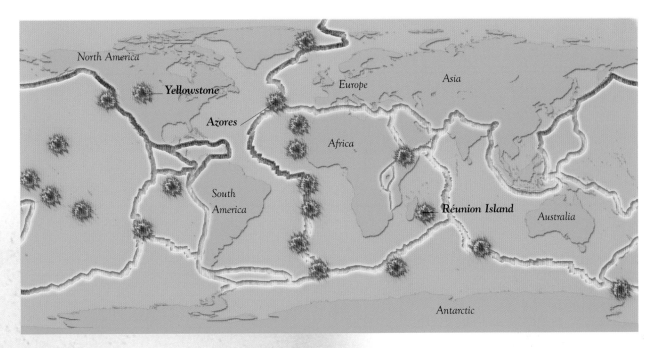

In the ocean

The thin plates at the bottom of the ocean are most easily pierced by hot magma. When this happens, an island is formed over the hot spot.

 Plate line   Hot spot

Underground oven

The Azores islands lie over a hot spot in the Atlantic Ocean. People here take advantage of the free underground heat and use it to cook their food.

This pot contains dinner for an Azores family.

Red-hot rivers

When a volcano erupts, hot liquid rock either explodes outward or flows onto the ground. Once it is outside of the volcano, the liquid rock can cause a lot of damage.

Exploding out

Sometimes the liquid rock is under a lot of pressure underground. When this happens, the lava spurts or explodes out of the volcano.

Destructive heat

Hot, liquid lava spreads out into rivers that can cover the countryside before it cools. It burns anything in its path, even roads.

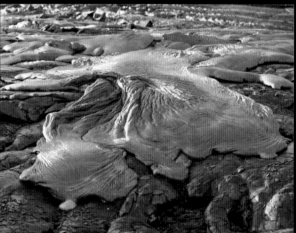

Slow but steady

When lava seeps out of the ground instead of exploding, it travels very slowly. Flowing lava is easier to run away from than exploding lava, but it is just as destructive to the landscape.

Aa and pahoehoe

There are many types of lava. Aa lava moves quickly and hardens to form sharp chunks. Pahoehoe lava moves slowly and often forms smooth rock when it hardens.

Aa rock is covered in sharp chunks and is difficult to walk over once it has cooled.

Pahoehoe lava flows grow a smooth skin.

As lava cools, it forms a hard "skin" over the liquid flow.

Lava facts

- The temperature of some lava is seven to 12 times hotter than boiling water.

- The words "aa" and "pahoehoe" come from the Hawaiian language.

- Lava can form many different shapes, such as cones, tubes, and even strands as fine as hair!

Glowing river

This intensely hot aa lava flow glows brightly. As it cools, the flow slows down and thickens, but since it cools very slowly, it can cover hundreds of miles before it stops.

Deadly blast

When a volcano explodes, gases inside the Earth escape with so much force that the lava is blasted into billions of tiny pieces. These pieces of rock come in all sizes, from huge boulders to fine dust.

Inside this cloud of ash there may be pieces of rock, gravel, and dust.

Steamy beginning
Steam can sometimes be seen escaping from the top or sides of a volcano. This is often the first sign that a volcano is active or may be getting ready to erupt.

Poisonous gas
Rocks and lava are dangerous, but the most deadly types of eruptions spew out tons of ash and poisonous gases that can cause death by suffocation.

No swimming!

Gases inside a volcano can also seep out slowly into lakes on the top or sides of the volcano. The gases can turn the lakes into pools of burning acid that dissolve skin and bone.

School crossing

Sakurajima volcano, in Japan, hurls lava rocks down onto the nearby town almost every day. For their protection, all the children on the island are required by law to wear hard hats to and from school.

The large rocks that are hurled from volcanoes are called bombs. Some bombs are as large as a house.

A gritty tale

Many forms of magma can be thrown from a volcano. Pumice is full of tiny bubbles of gas and is light enough to float. Smaller pieces are the size of gravel or dust.

Bomb

Gravel

Dust

Pumice

13

Volcanic weather

When a volcano erupts, huge amounts of dust and ash are thrown high up into the atmosphere. This debris can affect the weather all over the world, blocking out sunlight and turning summer days cold.

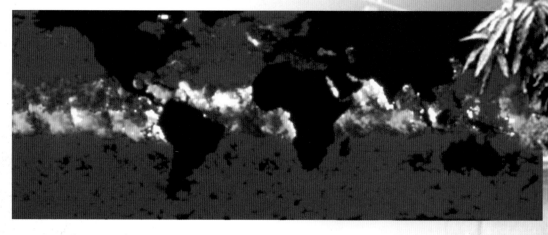

Traveling ash

This satellite photo was taken in 1991, one month after Mt. Pinatubo erupted in the Philippines. The light areas show the ash and dust from the volcano. It had already spread all around the world.

The eruption of Mt. Pinatubo lowered world temperatures by 1°F (0.5°C) for one year.

Lightning strikes

Lightning is often seen during eruptions. It is caused by tiny pieces of lava in an ash cloud rubbing against each other. The rubbing creates an electrical charge, which is lightning.

Turning day to night
When Mt. Pinatubo erupted, clouds of ash 25 miles (40 km) high blocked out the Sun. The land was dark and covered with gray ash.

In hot water

Water that is trapped underground near a volcano can get very hot. Sometimes the water turns into steam and shoots into the air as a geyser. At other times, it seeps up in pools called hot springs.

The water inside a geyser can be as much as three times hotter than the water boiling in a teakettle.

A rainbow of colors
This is the Fly Geyser in Nevada. The red cones formed when liquid minerals in the hot water cooled and turned solid. The yellow and green colors come from algae that live in the water.

Glorious mud

Underground heat from a volcano can even boil mud. This mud is rich in minerals and is often collected and used as a skin treatment. People bathe in the mud to make their skin soft and smooth.

Old Faithful shoots water between 100 and 165 ft (30–50 m) into the air.

Old Faithful

One of the most popular geysers in the world is Old Faithful in Yellowstone National Park. This geyser spurts faithfully every 78 minutes or so.

Fire under the sea

Under the sea, hot magma, chemicals, and minerals burn their way through thin spots in the Earth's plates. The lava and minerals bubble up to make islands and other unusual homes for undersea life.

Studying a hot subject

When lava erupts in water, it moves slowly and cools quickly. Scientists study underwater lava flows to learn more about how islands form.

LAVA DIVING

Because magma cools down quickly in water, experienced scuba divers can sometimes get a close-up look at small undersea eruptions.

Underwater chimneys

The minerals that rise to the ocean floor from deep in the Earth sometimes harden and make a chimney shape. These chimneys are called black smokers. Many unusual animals live in the warm, mineral-rich waters.

Black smoker facts

- Most black smokers are more than 1 mile (2 km) below the surface.

- The first black smoker was discovered in 1977.

- The animals living near black smokers include mussels, clams, and crabs.

Living on a chimney

Colorful tube worms live around black smokers. Special bacteria live inside these worms. They change the chemicals pouring out of the smokers into food.

This crab has made its home on the tube worms.

The volcanic seabed

Scientists believe there may be as many as 20,000 volcanoes under the sea. That's more than 90 percent of all the volcanoes on the planet. Many of the Earth's islands were formed from these undersea volcanoes.

This extinct volcano has stopped erupting.

An active volcano about to erupt under the ocean floor

Birth of an island

When a volcano erupts deep under the ocean, the lava piles up instead of flowing away. If the eruptions continue, the lava gradually builds up, until one day it breaks the surface and forms an island.

An island's birthday
In 1963, fishermen near Iceland saw a new island rise out of the water. The island was named Surtsey, after Surtur, the ancient Norse god of fire.

Three years later...
Once the lava flows stopped, plants and animals began to find their way to the new island. After just a few years, Surtsey was home to birds, grasses, and seals.

It takes millions of years for a volcano to reach the surface and become an island.

Underwater laboratory
As a new volcano grows toward the surface, it provides a home for a wide variety of marine life. This is why growing volcanoes are a great place to study undersea life.

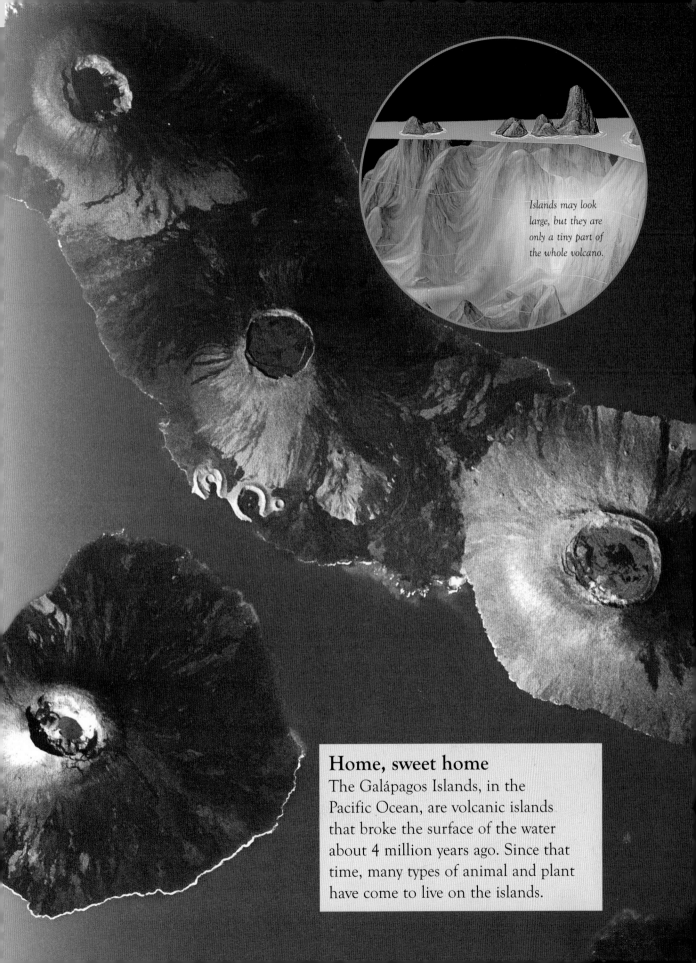

Islands may look large, but they are only a tiny part of the whole volcano.

Home, sweet home

The Galápagos Islands, in the Pacific Ocean, are volcanic islands that broke the surface of the water about 4 million years ago. Since that time, many types of animal and plant have come to live on the islands.

Tsunami

Many coastal towns' worst fear is a tsunami—a huge wave that destroys everything in its path. Many tsunamis are caused by volcanic eruptions.

Making waves

When a volcano erupts under the ocean, large parts of the ocean floor are lifted up, displacing water and creating a wave.

Landslide danger

Tsunamis are also caused when a large eruption sends huge amounts of lava and mud tumbling into the ocean.

At first, the displaced water is almost invisible as it travels quickly toward the shore.

A tsunami starts when a volcano erupts on the ocean floor.

Far out at sea, lava deep inside the Earth rises to the surface.

Tsunamis can travel up to 500 mph (805 kph) at sea.

Dangerous wave

Tsunamis can be even more dangerous than the eruptions that cause them. One of the deadliest tsunamis of all time was the 2004 Indian Ocean tsunami, although this was caused by a massive undersea earthquake and not a volcanic eruption.

City threatened

Huge tsunamis can sweep away entire towns and villages, flood hundreds of yards inland, and strip away beaches and vegetation.

When the tsunami reaches shallow water, it swells upward, forming a huge wave.

Water traveling back from the shore is also sucked up into the wave. A towering and terrifying tsunami is about to hit land!

Tsunami facts

● On May 21, 1792, Unzen volcano caused a tsunami that killed 14,300 people.

● The tallest recorded tsunami was 280 ft (85 m) high.

● The word tsunami means "harbor wave" in Japanese.

Diagram elements are not to scale.

Dead or alive?

Some volcanoes can seem to be dead, but they are only sleeping. A volcano that is not erupting, but might erupt again, is called dormant. A volcano that cannot erupt any more is called extinct.

Out of the blue

Mt. Pinatubo, in the Philippines, erupted in 1991 after lying dormant for 400 years. Ash and gas flowed along the ground at the speed of a car. The driver of this blue truck had to really put his foot down to escape.

In the shadow of Mt. Fuji

Mt. Fuji, in Japan, has been dormant since 1770, but it could come to life again at any time. This would be devastating for the 12 million people of Tokyo, 60 miles (97 km) away.

WAKING UP

Mt. Pinatubo began waking up in April 1991, when people heard rumbling sounds and saw steam and ash coming from the sides of the volcano. More than 200,000 people were quickly evacuated from the area. The volcano finally erupted in mid-July.

Starting to wake up

Scientists use satellites to keep a
close watch on dormant volcanoes.
The dots on these photos of Chiliques
volcano, in Chile, show where magma
is rising as the volcano wakes up.

*Infrared image of
Chiliques volcano*

*Satellite image of
Chiliques volcano*

On solid ground

This church in Le Puy, in
France, was built on the
remains of an old volcano.
The volcano is extinct and
will never erupt again.

Living in fear

Mount Etna, in Italy, is Europe's largest and most active volcano. The volcano has erupted at least 190 times in 3,500 years, but even so, thousands of people live and work on its slopes.

Blast from the past
One of the most dramatic eruptions of Mt. Etna was in 1669. Fifteen villages around the volcano were buried by lava, but no one was killed.

A pet's sixth sense
Some people who live near Mt. Etna watch the behavior of their pet cats to try to predict eruptions. Cats are very sensitive to changes in pressure that occur just before an eruption.

A constant threat

When Mt. Etna erupted in 2002, people living near the volcano were evacuated as the lava got close. It has erupted several times since then.

Early warning systems around Mt. Etna help people escape in time.

Build a barrier

The people living near Mt. Etna build barriers to help divert the flow of lava away from populated areas. During the 1669 eruption, the people of one town used rocks to divert the lava. Today, earth-moving machinery is used.

Luckily, Mt. Etna's lava flows very slowly.

Lava-land

There are more than 200 volcanoes in Iceland, which lies over a large hot spot in the Earth's crust. In January 1973, Eldfell volcano, on the island of Heimaey, erupted. The eruption continued for six months.

A curtain of fire

During the eruption of Eldfell, lava fountains spurted up from cracks in the volcano and formed a curtain of fire. Seawater was used to cool the lava and slow down the flow.

Buried homes

Most of Heimaey's 5,300 inhabitants were taken to Iceland's mainland and so escaped the eruption. Most of the island's buildings, however, were buried in black ash. Many of the buildings were later dug out and restored.

Eldfell means "fire mountain" in Icelandic. This fire mountain buried or destroyed more than 370 buildings.

A massive eruption

In March 2010, Eyjafjallajökull volcano, Iceland's sixth largest glacier, erupted. The eruption continued over a few months. It disrupted air traffic across Europe for several weeks and affected many people and businesses around the world.

A natural heat

The heat from Iceland's many volcanoes is put to good use. People bathe and relax in hot pools like this one, while the nearby power plant uses the heat from the water to make electricity.

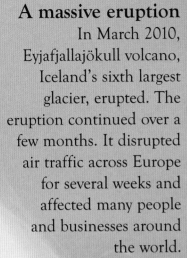

Mount St. Helens

One of the best-studied eruptions of all time occurred on May 18, 1980. That morning, Mount St. Helens, in the state of Washington, exploded in a fury of ash and smoke while scientists nearby took measurements.

Before 1980 eruption

After 1980 eruption

Blowing its top

Before the eruption, Mount St. Helens had a beautiful snow-capped peak. The blast tore off most of the north side of the volcano and left a huge, gaping hole big enough to fit an entire city into. This was the first time scientists had ever watched a volcano erupt from its side.

Huge explosion

Rocks, ash, volcanic gas, and steam blasted upward and outward faster than a jet plane and hotter than a furnace. Ash rose 15 miles (24 km) into the atmosphere in just 15 minutes.

The top 1,312 ft (400 m) of Mount St. Helens was blasted away.

A dreadful aftermath

The blast killed 57 people, destroyed wildlife and river valleys, and knocked down enough trees to build 300,000 homes.

A bottle of ash, please!

Ash from the eruption blocked out the sunlight for 250 miles (400 km) around. Later, the ash was bottled and sold as souvenirs.

Montserrat

The tiny island of Montserrat in the Caribbean was very peaceful until 1995. That year, Soufriere Hills volcano began erupting. Most of the residents have had to flee the island in fear for their lives.

Paradise regained

Montserrat was once a popular vacation spot. For a long time after the eruption the airport was buried under ash and tourists had to arrive by ferry, but life is now returning to normal.

Buried and deserted

In December 1997, Montserrat's capital city, Plymouth, was buried in 6½ ft (2 m) of mud and ash.

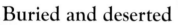

Time to rebuild

Some buildings, like this bell tower, survived the 1995 eruption and were dug out, but following the eruption in 1997, Plymouth was abandoned. A new capital, Little Bay, is now being developed.

Squeezed out

The people of Montserrat have been squeezed into smaller and smaller parts of their island as the volcano has taken over. There is now a large exclusion zone. The new capital of Little Bay is being developed in the northwest of the island.

Plymouth, former capital city

Little Bay

This area is the only part considered safe to inhabit.

Montserrat facts

● Around 8,000 people, two-thirds of the population, have left the island.

● Scientists think the Soufriere Hills volcano is about 100,000 years old.

● Since 1995, the eruptions have killed 20 people.

Land of fire

Indonesia lies in between two large plates. It is home to over 125 active volcanoes and has more recorded eruptions than any other country. Many of Indonesia's 15,000 islands were formed by volcanic activity.

Big bang
When Krakatau volcano erupted in 1883, the explosion was heard 2,500 miles (4,000 km) away in Alice Springs, Australia.

A beauty and a beast
Tengger Caldera is one of Indonesia's most visited volcanic areas. It's beauty masks a fiery heart—there have been more than 50 eruptions here in the last 200 years. It last erupted in 2011.

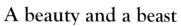

Mt. Bromo

Mt. Batok

Sulfur mining
Indonesia's many eruptions have brought valuable minerals close to the surface, where they are easy to mine. This man is carrying rocks of sulfur.

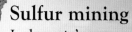

Since 1967, more than 600 people have been killed by Mt. Semeru.

Mt. Semeru

THE OGRE'S TASK

Legend says that Mt. Bromo was created when an ogre was ordered to dig a trench to win the hand of a princess. When the princess's angry father saw that the ogre might finish the trench, he ordered the ogre to speed up. The ogre died of exhaustion, and the half-coconut he used to dig the trench became Mt. Bromo.

Ancient tragedy

On the morning of August 24, 79 CE,
Mt. Vesuvius, in Italy, erupted. Hot ash,
dust, lava, and clouds of deadly gas
rained down on the people of Pompeii
and Herculaneum, burying both towns
for 1,600 years.

Preserved in ash
Pompeii is so well preserved that
it provides us with good evidence
of everyday life in an ancient
Roman town. Archeologists
can even read the graffiti
on the town's walls.

A Pompeiian victim
This man suffocated in the smoke and
ash of the eruption. His body later
decayed, leaving a hole. In modern
times, the hole was filled with
plaster to make a cast.

Sleeping, but not dead

Today, Mt. Vesuvius may look quiet, but the volcano has erupted about 36 times since 79 CE. The most recent eruption was in 1944 and lasted for 10 days. That time, only a few people were hurt.

The dog suffocated while chained to a post.

Died on duty

The cast shows a dog that died while he was guarding the house of his owner, a man named Vesonius Primus.

This guard dog was wearing a bronze collar.

This man tried to shield his face from the ash.

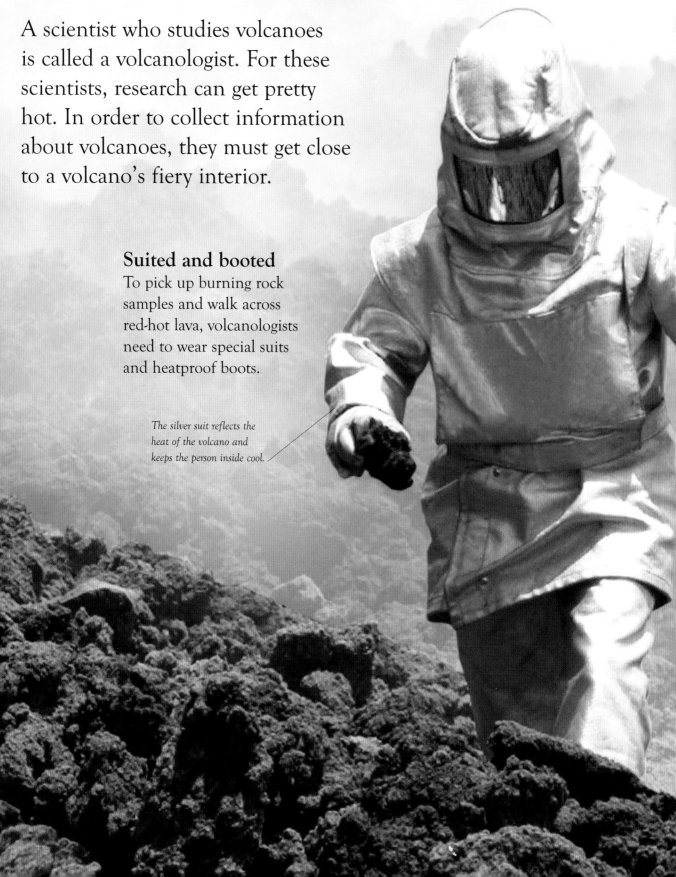

Work in the hot zone

A scientist who studies volcanoes is called a volcanologist. For these scientists, research can get pretty hot. In order to collect information about volcanoes, they must get close to a volcano's fiery interior.

Suited and booted
To pick up burning rock samples and walk across red-hot lava, volcanologists need to wear special suits and heatproof boots.

The silver suit reflects the heat of the volcano and keeps the person inside cool.

The camera provided scientists with a close-up view of a volcano's crater.

Robot on a mission

The Dante robot was once sent into volcanoes to gather information from places it was too dangerous for people to go. Its mission ended abruptly when it crashed during an expedition to a volcano in Antarctica.

Deadly gases

Even if it is not too hot, there may be invisible dangers in the form of deadly gases seeping from below ground. This is why gas masks are required equipment for volcanologists.

These volcanologists are taking samples of gas. The gas may give clues as to when the volcano will erupt next.

Visiting a volcano

Volcanoes are fascinating, and many people will go a long way to visit them. Each year, thousands of tourists travel to active volcanoes for the opportunity to get up close and personal with boiling lava.

It's safer up here

Some volcanoes can only be safely visited from the air. Hot lava and poisonous gases make it too dangerous to get any closer. These volcanoes are best toured by helicopter.

Stationary pool of hot lava

A spectacular display

Forget fireworks—a volcanic
sound and light show beats them
all! This volcano in Hawaii has
a small eruption almost every
night, and people hike for
several miles to watch it.

It is even possible to camp overnight near this active volcano in Hawaii.

VOLCANO PARK

Volcanoes National Park, on
the island of Hawaii, contains
one of the most active
volcanoes in the world—Kilauea.
Every year, thousands of tourists
visit the volcano, which has been
erupting continuously since 1983.

Weird and wonderful

Lava flows can form a large variety of weird and wonderful shapes when they cool. Sometimes, even scientists cannot explain how all these fantastic features were created!

Towering cones of lava
These structures in Pinnacles National Park, California, were formed 7,700 years ago by lava erupting from nearby Mt. Mazama.

Chimney houses

Hundreds of years ago, people hollowed out these volcanic chimneys in Cappadocia, Turkey, and used them as houses. People still live in some of them.

A road for giants

The people of ancient Ireland believed these rocks were the work of a giant named Finn McCool. The Giant's Causeway was actually created 60 million years ago by cooling lava flows.

Time to warm up

These Japanese monkeys have learned that soaking in a nearby volcanic hot spring makes a nice break from the winter chill and helps them to stay clean.

Animals also enjoy unusual volcanic areas.

Out of the ashes

Volcanic eruptions can bring devastation, but they can also bring renewal. Eruptions clear out old, dead plants, while the ash helps plants grow back more quickly and stronger than before.

Life returns

A few years after an eruption, plant life has returned to this volcano. The ash helps the plants grow quickly.

First sign of growth

Ferns have very tough seeds, so they are some of the first plants to push their way up through solid lava to start growing after an eruption.

Fertile slopes

Volcanic ash makes a great
fertilizer to help plants grow.
Farmers near this volcano in
Indonesia take advantage of
this by growing their crops all
the way up the sides and
into the crater of
this volcano.

Making a meal of it

Without volcanoes, people in
some of the poorest places in the
world would not have enough to
eat. Without the ash, the land
would not be fertile enough to
feed everyone.

Path to safety

Find a safe path through the hot lava by answering the questions correctly. Watch your step!

2,000

20,000

outer space

active

America

When **Krakatau** erupted in 1883, it could be heard in...
See page 34

A volcano that cannot **erupt** again is called...
See page 24

extinct

dormant

START

granite

Once **magma** has risen to the surface it's called...
See page 4

The **number** of
volcanoes in Iceland
is more than...
See page 28

FINISH

200

tsunamis

geysers

Australia

the same as the air outside

Huge waves
caused by **eruptions**
are called...
See page 22

hotter than boiling water

colder than ice

ash clouds

The **temperature**
of some lava is...
See page 11

lava

coal

True or false?

How much have you learned about volcanoes? Can you spot which of these statements are true and which are false?

Mt. Etna is Europe's smallest and least active volcano.
See pages 26–27

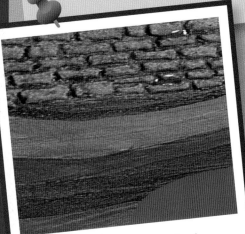

Igneous rocks are made from magma that has cooled.
See page 4

The Ring of Fire circles the Indian Ocean.
See pages 6–7

People in the Azores islands take advantage of the underground heat and use it to cook their food.
See page 9

When lava seeps out of the ground instead of exploding it travels very fast.
See page 10

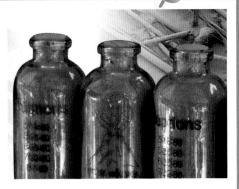

The lava collected from
the Mount St. Helens eruption
was bottled and sold
as souvenirs.
See page 31

Volcanologists wear special suits
to keep warm.
See page 38

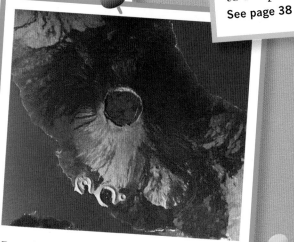

It takes about five years for a
volcano to reach the surface
and become an island.
See pages 20–21

Monkeys bathe in
volcanic hot springs.
See page 43

Plants can push their way
up through solid lava
to grow back.
See page 44

The Old Faithful geyser in the
US spurts every 78 minutes or so.
See page 17

Picture quiz

Are you hot on volcanoes?
Test yourself with this quiz.
All the answers can be
found in the book.

A scientist
who studies
volcanoes.
See page 38

This is the name
given to magma
once it rises to the
surface. It is so hot,
it can melt steel.
See page 4

This slow-moving
kind of lava forms a
smooth rock when
it hardens.
See page 10

These are
made from
rocks squashed
together.
See page 4

These are
created from
magma that
has cooled.
See page 4

This forms when a volcano explodes and gases inside the Earth escape. It contains pieces of rock, gravel, and dust.
See page 12

Tourists to the White Island volcano in New Zealand can walk right inside this part of the volcano.
See page 40

This is a fast-moving kind of lava. When is hardens, it forms sharp rocks.
See page 10

This layer of Earth is made of loose rocks and dirt. It is 3.5–42 miles (5.6–68 km) thick.
See pages 4–5

This is a thick liquid made of melted rocks, deep inside the Earth.
See page 4

These are made from pieces of rock squashed together.
See page 4

What's this?

Take a look at these close-ups of the pictures in the book and see if you can identify them. The clues should help you!

❮ This volcano has erupted 190 times in 3,500 years.

❮ Thousands of people work on its slopes.

See pages 26–27

❮ The ash collected from this volcano was sold as a souvenir.

❮ It erupted from its side.

See pages 30–31

❮ He suffocated in the smoke and ash of an eruption.

❮ His body decayed to leave a hole.

See pages 36–37

❮ It is named after the ancient Norse god of fire.

❮ It rose out of the water in 1963.

See page 20

❮ This was sent into volcanoes to gather information.

❮ It crashed on a visit to a volcano in Antarctica.

See page 39

❮ This underground heat fuels 10,000 geysers.

❮ A volcano erupted here two million years ago.

See page 8

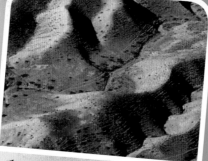

▸ People used to believe that a giant named Finn McCool created this.

▸ It was actually created by cooling lava flows.

See page 43

▸ This is located in the United States.

▸ This is where two plates slide against one other.

See page 7

▸ It is difficult to walk over it once it has cooled.

▸ It moves quickly and hardens to form sharp chunks.

See page 10

▸ It has erupted 36 times since 79 CE.

▸ This volcano is in Italy.

See pages 36–37

▸ People watch their behavior to predict eruptions.

▸ They are sensitive to changes in pressure.

See page 26

▸ Animals such as mussels, clams, and crabs live near them.

▸ The first one was discovered in 1977.

See page 19

Glossary

Here are the meanings of some words that are useful to know when learning about volcanoes.

Aa lava a crumbly, lumpy type of lava that moves slowly and can form tall flows.

Algae small, simple plants that live in water.

Ash very small, fine particles of lava that can block out sunlight.

Bacteria microscopic animals that can get their energy from chemicals.

Basalt the most common kind of volcanic rock, made from very runny lava.

Black smoker volcanic vent on the seafloor that belches out hot minerals.

Bomb big blob of lava that is thrown out by a volcano and cools in midair.

Chemical a natural substance made when different types of atom combine together.

Core the metallic center of the Earth.

Crater the part of a volcano that connects to the main chimney and out of which lava and ash erupts.

Crater lake a lake formed in the crater of a volcano.

Crust the hard, outer layer of the Earth.

Dormant a volcano that has not erupted for a long time, but could erupt again.

Eruption when lava, ash, or gas explode out of a volcano.

Extinct a volcano that cannot ever erupt again.

Fault a crack in the Earth's crust where rocks have moved.

Fissure a crack in the ground out of which runny lava oozes.

Geyser a place where underground water heated by magma spurts into the air.

Hot spot a place where rising magma burns through the Earth's crust.

Hot spring a place where hot water from under the ground bubbles to the surface.

Landslide the sliding of loose soil and rock down a steep slope.

Lava the name for magma that has erupted to the surface.

Magma rock deep in the Earth that has melted to a liquid.

Mantle the part of the Earth's interior that lies in between the crust and the core.

Metamorphic rock rock formed from other rocks that are under intense heat and pressure.

Mineral a natural substance that is not a plant or animal.

Mud pot a pool of hot, boiling mud.

Pahoehoe lava a hot, runny lava that moves freely in shallow flows.

Plate the moving part of the mantle and crust.

Rift a place where two plates are pulling apart to create a crack in the crust.

Ring of Fire an area in the Pacific Ocean that includes many of the world's most active and violent volcanoes.

Seismograph a machine that measures the movement of the Earth's surface.

Tsunami a destructive sea wave that can be caused by a volcanic eruption.

Volcanologist a scientist who studies volcanoes.

Index

Acknowledgments

Dorling Kindersley would like to thank:
Colin Bowler of Alan Collinson Design/Geo-Innovations, for map design, and Louise Halsey for her original volcano illustrations. Thanks, also, to the following DK staff: Jacqueline Gooden, Elinor Greenwood, Lorrie Mack, Fleur Star, Cheryl Telfer, and Sadie Thomas.

Picture credits

The publisher would like to thank the following for their kind permission to reproduce their photographs:
(Key: a-above; b-below/bottom; c-centre; f-far; l-left; r-right; t-top)

Mario Cipollini: 27tl; **Bruce Coleman Inc:** Stella Sneered 20cr; **Corbis:** 26-27c; Michael S. Lewis 52br; Yann Arthus-Bertrand 43b, 44-45, 49cr; Dan Bool/Sygma 34-35; Gary Braasch 31br; Carol Cohen 44c, 49bl; Sergio Dorantes 34tr; Chris Hellier 43tl; Ted Horowitz 44l; Michael S. Lewis 8tr; Ludovic Maisant 13tr; Pat O'Hara 42, 48; Robert Patrick 32tr, 32bl; Roger Ressmeyer 13c, 20bl, 36-37b, 39b, 40bl, 41b, 41t, 52c; Hans Georg Roth 9br, 48bl; Royalty-Free Images 24tr; Sean Sexton 37cr; Strauss/Curtis 45br; Kevin Schafer 44bl; Hans Strand 29cr; James A Sugar 31r;

Nick Wheeler 22c; Ralph White 19cr, 53bl; Adam Woolfit 25cr; **Ecoscene:** Wayne Lawler 48c; Lin Esposito: 36c; **GeoScience Features Picture Library:** 20tl; **Dreamstime.com:** Lucafabbian 53tl; **Getty Images:** Barcroft Media 29tr, G. Brad Lewis/The Image Bank 48br; Tom Pfeiffer/VolcanoDiscovery/Photographer's Choice 52tr, 53br; Astromujoff/Riser 49cl; Warren Bolster 22-23c; Michael Dunning 22tr; Jack Dykinga 16-17; G. Brad Lewis 10cr, 46-47; NASA 21c; Guido Alberto Rossi 12cl; Schafer & Hill 22l; Pete Turner 28-29, 29tr; Greg Vaughn 2-3; Art Wolfe 12-13c; **Robert Harding Picture Library:** 10tr, 10cl, 11; Photri 30cl; E. Simanor 43tr; Katz/FSP: 14cl, 24-25; R. Gaillarde/Gamma 8-9; **NASA:** 5tr, 25tl, 25tc, 33tr; **Photoshot:** Stella Snead 52bl; **Panos Pictures:** Rob Huibers 32-33; Chris and Helen Pellant: 17tl; **Popperfoto:** Tony Gentile/Reuters 1; Reuters 38; **Powerstock Photolibrary:** Superstock 13br; **Reuters:** Mario Laporta 49tr, 50cl; **Rex Features:** Sipa Press 15; **Science Photo Library:** 30-31; Bernhard Edmaier 2tc, 4-5c, 7tr, 34bl; **NASA/Carnegie Mellon University** 39tr, 52cl, 52bc; Mark Newman 14bc; David Parker 7tl, 53tc; **Seapics.com:** Doug Perrine 18; Verena Tunnicliffe: 19tr; **US Geological Survey:** Lyn Topinka, United States Department of the Interior, U.S Geological Survey, David A. Johnston Cascades Volcano Observatory, Vancouver, Washington 30cr.

All other images © Dorling Kindersley
For further information see: www.dkimages.com